FRESH FROM THE OVEN

CAKES & SPONGES

HARBOUR
BOOKS

CONTENTS

ALMOND BUTTER RING

1/4 cup (1 oz, 30 g) flaked almonds, for coating
8 oz (250 g) butter, softened
2 1/2 cups (16 oz, 500 g) superfine (caster) sugar
1 teaspoon vanilla extract (essence)
1/2 teaspoon almond extract (essence)
5 eggs
2 1/2 cups (10 oz, 315 g) all-purpose (plain) flour
1/4 teaspoon double-acting baking powder (1/2 teaspoon baking powder)
1/2 teaspoon baking soda (bicarbonate of soda)
1/4 teaspoon salt
3/4 cup (6 fl oz, 180 ml) sour cream

Preheat oven to 325°F (160°C, Gas Mark 3). Well grease a 9 inch (23 cm) fluted ring cake tin and scatter almonds over the surface, pressing on lightly; dust a little flour over all, shaking off surplus.

Beat the butter, caster sugar, vanilla, and almond extract until very light and frothy. Add the eggs one at a time, beating well after each addition.

Sift dry ingredients together, then sift over butter-egg mixture and fold in. Add sour cream and fold through lightly but thoroughly. Spoon cake mixture into the cake tin.

Bake for 1 1/2 to 1 3/4 hours. Remove from oven and stand for 5 to 6 minutes before turning out onto a cake rack to cool.

If desired dust the cake lightly with sifted caster and confectioners' sugar before serving.

AMBROSIA CAKE

³/4 cup (6 fl oz, 180 ml) mashed banana (1 large banana)
1¹/4 cups (8 oz, 250 g) sugar
¹/2 cup (4 fl oz, 125 ml) corn oil
2 eggs, lightly beaten
1¹/2 tablespoons grated orange rind
2¹/3 cups (9¹/2 oz, 300 g) all-purpose (plain) flour
³/4 teaspoon baking soda (bicarbonate of soda)
¹/2 teaspoon double-acting baking powder (1 teaspoon baking powder)
¹/4 teaspoon salt
³/4 cup (6 fl oz, 180 ml) orange juice
2 cups (16 fl oz, 500 ml) heavy (double) cream
1 cup (8 oz, 250 g) canned crushed pineapple
2 tablespoons Southern Comfort or peach brandy
1 cup (4 oz, 125 g) shredded (desiccated) coconut

Cream together banana, sugar, corn oil, eggs, and orange rind. Add flour, baking soda, baking powder, salt, and orange juice and mix well.

Preheat oven to 350°F (180°C, Gas Mark 4). Lightly butter and flour two 9 inch (22.5 cm) round layer cake tins or a 13 x 9 x 2 inch (32.5 x 22.5 x 5 cm) slab cake tin. Pour in the batter and bake until the top springs back when touched in the middle, about 30 minutes for layers or 40 minutes for a slab cake. Cool in the tin for about 10 minutes, then turn out on a rack to cool completely.

To make a layer cake, whip half of the cream and fold in all the pineapple. Spread between the layers. Whip the remainder of the cream with the liqueur and spread over the top and sides. Sprinkle the top with coconut. To make a slab cake, whip all the cream, fold in the pineapple and liqueur, spread over the top and sides and top with coconut. Chill for about an hour before serving.

APPLE PURÉE FRUIT CAKE

SERVES 12-24

6 large green cooking apples
1 cup (8 oz, 250 g) polyunsaturated margarine
2 cups (1 lb, 500 g) raw sugar
3 cups (12 oz, 375 g) all-purpose wholewheat (plain wholemeal) flour
1 tablespoon baking soda (bicarbonate of soda)
1 teaspoon ground cinnamon
1 teaspoon mixed spice
2 cups (12 oz, 375 g) seedless raisins, or 1 cup of seedless raisins and
1 of golden raisins (sultanas)
¹/₃ cup (2 oz, 60 g) mixed peel
¹/₃ cup (2 oz, 60 g) glacé cherries, chopped
¹/₂ cup (2 oz, 60 g) filberts (hazelnuts), chopped

Peel, core, and slice apples, stew with 1 tablespoon water, then mix to a purée when cool. Measure 2¹/₂ cups (20 fl oz, 600 ml) purée and pour into a pan. Add margarine and sugar and heat gently, stirring until sugar is dissolved.

Sift flour, baking soda, and spices into a mixing bowl, and make a "well" in the middle. Pour apple mixture into well and stir until combined. Stir in raisins, mixed peel, cherries, and nuts.

Put mixture in a lined, greased 9 inch (23 cm) round cake tin and bake at 350°F (190°C, Gas Mark 5) for 1¹/₂ hours, or until cooked. Test with a warm skewer. Stand in tin for at least 10 minutes before turning out. Cool on a wire cooling tray.

BANANA PECAN COFFEE CAKE

SERVES 8

2 cups (16 oz, 500 g) mashed bananas (3 large bananas)
3 1/2 cups (14 oz, 440 g) all-purpose (plain) flour
2 teaspoons double-acting baking powder (4 teaspoons baking powder)
2/3 cup (5 oz, 155 ml) vegetable oil
1 1/3 cups (9 oz, 270 g) sugar
2 eggs
2/3 cup (3 oz, 90 g) chopped pecans

PRALINE TOPPING:
1/4 cup (2 oz, 60 g) butter
1 cup (8 oz, 250 g) packed brown sugar
1/4 cup (1 oz, 30 g) all-purpose (plain) flour
1/2 teaspoon grated nutmeg
1 cup (4 oz, 125 g) pecan halves

Preheat oven to 350°F (180°C, Gas Mark 4). Thoroughly mix all the cake ingredients and spread in an oiled 13 x 9 x 2 inch (32.5 x 22.5 x 5 cm) cake tin.

Topping: Melt the butter in a saucepan over medium heat. Stir in sugar, flour, nutmeg, and pecans. Smooth the praline mixture over the batter. Decorate with pecan halves. Bake for 1 hour or until a tester inserted in the middle comes out clean. Cool before serving.

BASIC BUTTER CAKE

4 oz (125 g) butter or margarine, softened
¹/₂ cup (4 oz, 125 g) sugar
1 teaspoon vanilla essence
2 eggs
2 cups (8 oz, 250 g) self-raising flour
¹/₄ teaspoon salt
¹/₂ cup (4 fl oz, 125 ml) milk

Preheat the oven to 325°F (160°C, Gas Mark 3). Grease an 8 inch (20 cm) cake tin.

Beat butter and sugar with vanilla until light and creamy. Add eggs one at a time, beating well after each addition.

Sift the flour and salt together. Sift and fold into butter-sugar-eggs mixture in alternate batches with the milk, adding about a third of each at a time; mix lightly but thoroughly.

Spoon into cake tin and bake in the oven for 55 to 60 minutes. Remove and allow to stand for 3 to 7 minutes before turning out onto a cake rack to cool.

Ice with flavored icing of your choice.

BUTTERED COTTAGE TWISTS

2 eggs
1 cup (8 oz, 250 g) sugar
1/2 cup (4 oz, 125) cottage cheese
1/2 cup (4 fl oz, 125 ml) maize oil
1 teaspoon grated lemon rind
1 teaspoon vanilla extract (essence)
4 cups (1 lb, 500 g) all-purpose (plain) flour, sifted
1 teaspoon baking soda (bicarbonate of soda)
1/2 cup (4 fl oz, 125 ml) milk
2–3 tablespoons sesame seeds
butter or margarine, for spreading

Preheat oven to 400°F (200°C, Gas Mark 6). Grease a 9¹/₂ x 2¹/₂ inch (24 x 6 cm) bar tin.

Reserve one egg white for glazing. Combine the other egg white and yolks with sugar, and beat until fluffy. Add cottage cheese, oil, lemon rind, and vanilla, and beat well. Fold in the sifted flour and baking soda, add the milk and mix to a soft dough — use a little extra milk if the mixture seems too firm.

Turn onto a lightly floured board; divide the dough into four and knead each to a thin strip about 12 inches (30 cm) long. Taking two of the strips, twist loosely together and lift into the bar tin. Repeat with the other two strips. Leave space between the two twists — the dough will rise during baking. Lightly beat the reserved egg white and brush over the twists; sprinkle sesame seeds on top.

Bake for 8 to 10 minutes, then reduce the temperature to moderate, 350°F (180°C, Gas Mark 4), and bake for a further 25 to 30 minutes. Turn out and serve warm in buttered slices.

CHOCOLATE PRUNE CAKE

1 cup (7 oz, 220 g) whole prunes
4 oz (125 g) butter
1 cup (6 oz, 185 g) brown sugar
2 eggs
1 cup (4 oz, 125 g) self-rising (raising) flour
1 cup (4 oz, 125 g) self-rising (raising) wholewheat (wholemeal) flour
1/2 cup (2 oz, 60 g) cocoa
1/2 teaspoon ground cloves
1/2 cup (4 fl oz, 125 ml) prune-cooking water

CHOCOLATE ICING:

1 1/2 cups (8 oz, 250 g) icing (confectioner's) sugar
1–2 tablespoons cocoa or drinking chocolate
1/2 oz (15 g) butter or margarine
1–2 tablespoons water, boiling

Preheat oven to 350°F (180°C, Gas Mark 4). Grease an 8 x 6 inch (20 x 15 cm) square pan (tin).

Gently simmer prunes in 2 cups (16 fl oz, 500 ml) water for 8 minutes. Cool, and drain, saving liquid. Remove stones.

Beat butter and sugar until creamy. Add eggs, and beat until well combined. Sift in flours, cocoa, and cloves. Stir in prunes, adding 1/2 cup (4 fl oz, 125 ml) of prune cooking liquid. Pour into pan. Bake for 40 minutes. Cool in pan.

While cake is cooling, prepare the chocolate icing.

Chocolate Icing: Sift the icing sugar and cocoa or drinking chocolate into a bowl; make a well in the center.

Melt the butter in about 1 1/2 tablespoons of boiling water. Add this to the icing sugar, and stir to smooth consistency. Add drops of boiling water, as required, to blend to creamy consistency. Pour at once onto the cake, and smooth over with a broad knife or spatula. Allow to set before cutting.

Chocolate Prune Cake with Walnuts and Coffee Icing: Add 1/2 cup (2 oz, 60 g) of chopped walnuts to batter when mixing the cake. To make coffee icing, substitute 1–2 teaspoons of instant coffee powder or coffee essence for the cocoa or drinking chocolate. Proceed as for chocolate icing; sprinkle with ground walnut.

CHOCOLATE SLICE

1 1/2 cups (6 oz, 185 g) all-purpose (plain) flour

2 tablespoons cocoa

3/4 cup (6 oz, 185 g) sugar

1/4 teaspoon salt

1/2 teaspoon double-acting baking powder (1 teaspoon baking powder)

1/3 cup (3 fl oz, 90 ml) maize oil

1 tablespoon vinegar

1 teaspoon vanilla extract (essence)

1 cup (8 fl oz, 250 ml) water, just lukewarm

CHOCOLATE BUTTER CREAM:

3 oz (90 g) butter or margarine

1 cup (6 oz, 185 g) semi-sweet (dark) chocolate pieces

1/2 cup (4 fl oz, 125 g) sour cream

1 teaspoon vanilla extract (essence) or rum extract (essence)

2 1/2 –2 3/4 cups (14–16 oz, 440–500 g) confectioners' (icing) sugar

Preheat oven to 350°F (180°C, Gas Mark 4). Line and grease a 9 inch (23 cm) slab tin.

Sift flour, cocoa, sugar, salt, and baking powder twice, then sift into the mixing bowl and make a well in the middle.

Mix oil and vinegar with the vanilla extract and water, and beat to combine. Pour into the flour-cocoa mixture. Using a flat egg whisk, beat as quickly and lightly as possible to combine — do not "overbeat". Turn into the slab tin.

Bake for 30 to 35 minutes or until springy to the touch. Remove from oven and stand for 5 to 6 minutes before turning out onto a cake rack to cool.

Cover with chocolate butter cream and, when set, cut into slices or shapes for serving.

Chocolate butter cream: Combine butter and chocolate pieces in a heatproof bowl over hot, not boiling water, and stir until blended. Remove from heat and cool slightly.

Stir in sour cream and vanilla or rum extract, and gradually work in sifted confectioners' sugar to form a soft, spreading consistency; beat well. Use as a filling between the layers and to cover the cake; swirl or peak the top into an attractive design. Allow to become firm before cutting.

CIDER HONEY LUNCHEON CAKE

1 cup (4 oz, 125 g) all-purpose (plain) flour
1 cup (4 oz, 125 g) wholewheat (wholemeal) flour
1 teaspoon mixed spices
$^1/_4$ teaspoon salt
$^1/_4$ teaspoon ground ginger
$^1/_2$ cup (3 oz, 90 g) golden raisins (sultanas)
2 tablespoons (1 oz) chopped mixed peel
$^1/_4$ cup (1$^1/_2$ oz, 45 g) brown sugar
4 oz (125 g) butter or margarine, melted
$^2/_3$ cup (7 oz, 220 g) honey
1 teaspoon baking soda (bicarbonate of soda)
5 fl oz (150 ml) sparkling cider
1 egg, beaten

Preheat oven to 325°F (160°C, Gas Mark 3). Line and grease a 9 x 4$^1/_2$ inch (23 x 12 cm) loaf pan (tin).

Combine hot melted butter with honey, and pour into the well.

Dissolve baking soda in cider, and quickly add this and beaten egg to bowl. Beat all ingredients together with a flat egg whisk until mixed thoroughly. Turn into loaf pan.

Bake for 55 to 60 minutes. Take out of oven and stand for 5 to 6 minutes before carefully turning onto a cake rack. When cold, store in airtight container for 1 to 2 days before slicing.

COCONUT CAKE

3 1/2 cups (14 oz, 440 g) all-purpose (plain) flour
pinch of salt
2 teaspoons double-acting baking powder (4 teaspoons baking powder)
8 oz (250 g) butter
1 1/4 cups (10 oz, 315 g) superfine (caster) sugar
1/2 cup (2 oz, 60 g) shredded (desiccated) coconut
1/3 cup grated solidified coconut milk
4 eggs, beaten
3/4 cup (6 fl oz, 185 ml) milk

GLACÉ ICING:
1 1/2 cups (8 oz, 250 g) confectioners' (icing) sugar
1/2 oz (15 g) butter or margarine
1–2 tablespoons water
1 tablespoon shredded coconut

Preheat oven to 350°F (180°C, Gas Mark 4). Grease an 8 inch (20 cm) cake tin, and line with waxed (greaseproof) paper.

Sift flour, salt, and baking powder into a large bowl. Rub in butter until mixture resembles fine breadcrumbs. Stir in sugar, coconut, and grated coconut milk. Gradually mix the eggs and milk into the flour mixture. Turn it into the cake tin and smooth the top.

Bake for 1 1/2 to 1 3/4 hours. Turn out onto a wire rack to cool. The cake can be decorated with glacé icing, sprinkled with shredded coconut.

Glacé Icing: Sift the sugar into a bowl; make a well in the middle. Heat 1 1/2 tablespoons of the water.

Melt butter in the warm water, add to sugar, and stir to smooth consistency. Add drops of the remaining water to blend to creamy consistency. Pour at once onto the cake, and smooth over with a broad knife or spatula. Sprinkle with the shredded coconut.

Leave to set before cutting.

CRUSTED CHOCOLATE CAKE

4 oz (125 g) butter or margarine, softened
9 oz (1²/3 cup) brown sugar
2 eggs, separated
4 oz (125 g) unsweetened (cooking) chocolate, melted
1 cup (6 oz, 180 g) chopped raisins
2 cups (10 oz, 300 g) all purpose (plain) flour
3 teaspoons baking powder
¹/2 teaspoon cinnamon
¹/2 cup (4 fl oz, 125 ml) sour milk
¹/4 cup (2 fl oz, 60 ml) brandy, warmed
1–2 tablespoons white sugar, for topping

Preheat oven to 350°F (180°C, Gas Mark 4). Line and grease a deep sided 8 inch (20 cm) cake tin.

Beat the butter and 1¹/3 cups (7 oz, 210 g) of the sugar until light and fluffy.

Beat the egg yolks with the remaining ¹/3 cup (2 oz, 60 g) of sugar, then beat the two mixtures together. Add the cooled chocolate and raisins; mix thoroughly.

Sift the dry ingredients together.

Combine the sour milk and brandy. Add alternate batches of the milk-brandy and flour mixtures to the butter-chocolate mixture.

Beat the egg whites until soft peaks form, and fold very lightly into the cake mixture — do not overmix. Spoon into the cake tin and sprinkle the white sugar over the top.

Bake in the preheated oven for 40 minutes, then lower the temperature slightly and bake for a further 40 to 50 minutes. Remove from the oven and allow to stand for 8 to 10 minutes before carefully turning out onto a wire rack to cool.

DUNDEE CAKE

8 oz (250 g) butter
1 cup (6 oz, 185 g) superfine (caster) sugar
2 oranges
5 eggs
2¹/₂ cups (10 oz, 315 g) all-purpose (plain) flour
¹/₂ teaspoon double-acting baking powder (1 teaspoon baking powder)
pinch salt
¹/₂ cup (3 oz, 90 g) almonds
1 cup (5 oz, 155 g) golden raisins (sultanas)
1 cup (5 oz, 155 g) currants
¹/₂ cup (3 oz, 90 g) chopped mixed peel
extra blanched almonds

Grease an 8 inch (20 cm) round cake tin. Line tin with one thickness of brown and one thickness of waxed (greaseproof) paper. Preheat oven to 300°F (150°C, Gas Mark 2).

Cream butter and sugar with grated rind of the oranges. Beat in eggs, one at a time. Sift flour, baking powder, and salt. Blanch and chop almonds. Mix into the flour with the fruit. Stir into the creamed mixture with 1 tablespoon orange juice. Turn into the tin. Smooth the top and arrange extra blanched almonds in a pattern on the top. Bake for about 2 to 2¹/₂ hours or until a skewer inserted in middle comes out clean. Cool in the tin.

FRESH APPLE CAKE

1 cup (6 oz, 185 g) brown sugar
2 eggs
1/2 cup (4 fl oz, 125 ml) vegetable oil
1 teaspoon vanilla extract (essence)
3 tablespoons milk
4 apples, cored and diced
2 cups (8 oz, 250 g) wholewheat (wholemeal) flour
1/2 teaspoon double-acting baking powder (1 teaspoon baking powder)
1/2 teaspoon salt
1/2 teaspoon ground cinnamon
1/2 teaspoon grated nutmeg

Preheat oven to 350°F (180°C, Gas Mark 4). Grease and flour a 9 inch (22 cm) square cake tin.

Beat together the sugar and eggs until thick and light. Beat in the oil and vanilla and milk. Stir in the diced apple.

In a separate bowl sift together flour, baking powder, salt, and spices, then fold into the apple mixture. Pour into the cake tin.

Bake for 45 minutes. Serve warm, with hot custard or with a yogurt and honey mix if desired.

HAZELNUT COFFEE CAKE

6 oz (185 g) butter or margarine, softened
³/₄ cup (6 oz, 185 g) superfine (caster) sugar
1 teaspoon instant coffee powder
1 tablespoon (1 oz, 30 g) honey
4 eggs
1 tablespoon whiskey coffee cream liqueur
1 ¹/₄ cups (4 oz, 125 g) ground filberts (hazelnuts)
1 cup (4 oz, 125 g) self-raising flour

COFFEE FUDGE FROSTING:

²/₃ cup (5 ¹/₂ fl oz, 160 ml) evaporated milk
1 cup (8 oz, 300 g) sugar
2 oz (60 g) butter or margarine
1 teaspoon coffee essence
2 teaspoons whiskey-coffee cream liqueur

Preheat oven to 350°F (180°C, Gas Mark 4). Grease and flour a deep-sided 8 inch (20 cm) springform cake tin or fluted ring tin.

Beat butter and sugar until creamy. Add instant coffee powder and honey, beat until light and fluffy. Add eggs one at a time, beating well after each addition. Beat the liqueur in well, and fold the filberts (hazelnuts) through.

Sift flour over the butter-filbert mixture and fold through lightly. Spoon into the springform tin. Bake for 45 to 50 minutes. Remove from oven and stand for 5 to 6 minutes before loosening the cake tin ring. When cold, put the cake on a serving plate.

To make the frosting, place the evaporated milk, sugar, butter and coffee essence in a nonstick saucepan and heat slowly until the sugar is dissolved; stir gently to blend.

Bring to a boil; then boil steadily until, when a teaspoon of mixture is dropped into a glass of cold water, a soft ball is formed — about 5 minutes. Take the saucepan from the heat and stand it in a large (heatproof) bowl containing iced water, to immediately retard further cooking. Beat constantly with a wooden spoon until the mixture commences to thicken. Remove the saucepan from the bowl.

Add the liqueur, and continue beating to a soft whipped-cream consistency. Pour onto the cake, allowing the frosting to drizzle down the sides. Allow to set before cutting.

LATTICED APPLE CAKE

6 oz (185 g) butter or margarine, softened
³/4 cup (6 oz, 185 g) sugar
1 teaspoon grated lemon rind
4 eggs
2¹/4 cups (9 oz, 270 g) all-purpose (plain) flour
1 teaspoon double-acting baking powder (2 teaspoons baking powder)

TOPPING:

1 cup (6 oz, 185 g) drained cooked (or canned) apples
1–2 tablespoons sugar (optional)

ALMOND PASTE:

1 cup (5 oz, 155 g) confectioners' (icing) sugar
¹/4 cup (2 oz, 60 g) ground almonds or almond meal
1 egg yolk
1 teaspoon sweet sherry
dash lemon juice
1–2 tablespoons confectioners' (icing) sugar

Preheat oven to 350°F (180°C, Gas Mark 4). Grease and flour an 8 inch (20 cm) springform tin.

Beat butter and sugar with the lemon rind until creamy. Add eggs one at a time, beating well after each addition. Sift flour and baking powder over the cream mixture and fold through. Spread into the springform tin and level the surface.

Bake for 35 to 40 minutes. Remove from oven and leave in the tin for 5 to 6 minutes before adding the topping.

Topping: Sweeten the apples with sugar, if desired.

Almond paste: Sift the sugar into a bowl and add the ground almonds; mix thoroughly and make a well in the middle. Beat the egg yolk, sweet sherry, and lemon juice together; pour into sugar mixture and gradually work into a firm smooth paste with one hand, kneading well.

Lightly sprinkle a board or work bench with a little extra confectioners' sugar, lift the mixture onto the board, and knead with both hands to a firm smooth dough — do not add too much extra icing sugar unless the dough is very soft. Cover tightly until ready for use, then re-knead gently before rolling out and applying to the cake as required.

Roll out the almond paste to about 1/4 inch (5 mm) thickness and cut into ³/4 inch (2 cm) strips. Carefully spread apples over the still-warm cake and arrange a lattice pattern of almond paste strips on top. Drop a little apricot jam between the lattice pieces.

Return to oven for a further 15 to 20 minutes. Remove from springform tin and cool; dust with confectioners' sugar before serving.

LEMON COCONUT CAKE

¹/₂ cup (4 oz, 125 g) unsalted butter or margarine
1 cup (8 oz, 250 g) superfine (caster) sugar
4 large eggs
2 cups (6 oz, 185 g) unsweetened shredded (desiccated) coconut
1 cup (4 oz, 125 g) self-raising flour, sifted

SYRUP:

1 cup (8 oz, 250 g) sugar
¹/₂ cup (4 fl oz, 125 ml) water
finely grated rind and juice of 1 lemon
1 teaspoon rosewater, optional

Cream butter and sugar until light and fluffy. Add eggs one at a time and beat well after each addition. Gently stir in coconut and flour until combined. Put mixture into a base-lined and greased 8 inch (20 cm) round cake tin and bake at 325°F (160°C, Gas Mark 3) for 1 hour or until cooked.

Syrup: Bring all ingredients to a boil, stirring until sugar is dissolved. Pour syrup over cake as soon as it comes out of the oven. Leave cake to cool in tin before turning out.

MAHOGANY CAKE WITH PECAN FUDGE FROSTING

³/₄ cup (6 oz, 185 g) sweetened cocoa powder
1 cup (8 oz, 250 g) packed brown sugar
¹/₂ cup (4 fl oz, 125 ml) molasses
1 cup (8 fl oz, 250 ml) boiling water
³/₄ cup (6 fl oz, 180 ml) corn oil
3 eggs
2 tablespoons dark rum
2¹/₂ cups (12 oz, 375 g) all-purpose (plain) flour
2 teaspoons baking powder (bicarbonate of soda)
¹/₂ teaspoon salt
1 teaspoon cinnamon

FROSTING:

3 oz (90 g) unsweetened (cooking) chocolate
3 tablespoons butter
2 tablespoons molasses
5 tablespoons cream
3 cups (8 oz, 250 g) confectioners' (icing) sugar
pecan halves or finely chopped pecans for garnish

Preheat oven to 350°F (180°C, Gas Mark 4). Mix cocoa, brown sugar, molasses, and boiling water; cool. Beat in the oil, eggs, rum, flour, baking soda, salt, and cinnamon.

Butter and flour an 8 or 9 inch (20 or 22.5 cm) round cake tin or a 13 x 9 x 2 inch (32.5 x 22.5 x 5 cm) slab cake tin. Pour batter into cake tin and bake about 25 minutes for layers, 40 minutes for a slab cake, until cake springs back lightly when pressed in the middle.

Frosting: Melt chocolate and butter in a double saucepan or in the microwave (about 1¹/₂ minutes on HIGH). Add molasses and beat in the cream and sugar, alternating 1 tablespoon cream with ¹/₂ cup (¹/₃ oz, 40 g) confectioners' sugar. Spread on cooled cake. Decorate with pecan halves or finely chopped pecans.

MANDARIN MUESLI CHEESECAKE

CRUMB CRUST:

2 cups (10 oz, 315 g) muesli, non-toasted variety

1/2 cup wholewheat (wholemeal) cookie (biscuit) crumbs

1 tablespoon soy compound

1/4 cup (1 oz, 30 g) ground filberts (hazelnuts)

1 teaspoon ground cinnamon

1 teaspoon ground nutmeg

1/4 teaspoon ground cloves

5 oz (155 g) unsalted butter or polyunsaturated margarine, melted

FILLING:

10 oz (315 g) can mandarins

2 eggs

3/4 cup (6 oz, 185 g) raw sugar

1/6 oz (5 g) agar agar

12 oz (375 g) cream cheese

10 fl oz (300 ml) cream

passionfruit and pistachio nuts for decoration

Crumb crust: Mix all ingredients together until well combined. Press over the bottom and up the sides of a greased 9 inch (23 cm) springform tin. Chill in the refrigerator until set.

Filling: Drain mandarins, reserve juice and make up to 1 cup (8 fl oz, 250 ml) with water. Put 1 egg, 1 egg yolk, and sugar in the top of a double-boiler and beat with a wire whisk over gently bubbling water until thick and creamy. Cool to blood heat (lukewarm).

Soak agar agar with reserved juice and water in a pan then simmer gently for 15 minutes or until dissolved. Cool to blood heat. Whisk agar agar into egg custard while both are at blood heat.

Sieve cream cheese into a mixing bowl, add egg custard mixture and mandarins and fold together. Whip two-thirds of cream and whisk egg white. Fold into cheese mixture, reserving a third of cream for decoration.

Pour filling into crumb crust and chill in refrigerator until set. Loosen crust carefully from side of tin with a palette knife before serving.

Serve decorated with remaining cream, whipped, passionfruit and chopped pistachio nuts.

RICH CHOCOLATE BUTTER CAKE

2 inch (5 cm) strip of vanilla pod
$^1/_2$ cup (4 fl oz, 125 ml) milk, hot
6 oz (185 g) unsweetened (cooking) chocolate, chopped
6 oz (185 g) butter, softened
$^3/_4$ cup (6 oz, 185 g) superfine (caster) sugar
4 eggs, separated
1 cup (4 oz, 125 g) all-purpose (plain) flour
$^1/_2$ cup (2 oz, 60 g) cornstarch (cornflour)
$^1/_2$ teaspoon double-acting baking powder (1 teaspoon baking powder)
$^1/_2$ teaspoon baking soda (bicarbonate of soda)

FROSTING:
4 oz (125 g) block fruit and nut chocolate
1 oz (30 g) butter
$^1/_4$ cup (2 fl oz, 60 ml) evaporated milk
$^1/_2$ cup (3 oz, 90 g) confectioners' (icing) sugar, sifted

Infuse the vanilla pod in the hot milk for 30 minutes. Preheat oven to 350°F (180°C, Gas Mark 4). Line the base of a deep-sided 8 inch (20 cm) cake tin, and grease it well.

Discard the vanilla pod, and add chocolate to the now vanilla-flavored milk. Over a very low heat, stir in 1 oz (30 g) of the butter until well blended. Allow to cool.

Beat remaining butter with the sugar until light and fluffy. Add cooled chocolate mixture and beat well. Add egg yolks one at a time and mix in lightly. Sift the dry ingredients together, then sift them over the butter-chocolate mixture and fold in lightly. Beat egg whites until they form stiff peaks then gently fold into the mixture — do not overmix. Turn into the cake tin.

Bake for 60 to 80 minutes. Remove from oven and stand for 5 to 6 minutes before carefully turning out onto a cake rack to cool.

When cold, wrap a "collar" of waxed (greaseproof) paper around the cake, so that the top edge of the paper stands about 1 inch (2.5 cm) above the surface of the cake.

Frosting: Chop the block of chocolate into small pieces, and melt with the butter in a heatproof basin placed over hot, not boiling, water. Remove from heat, and stir in evaporated milk and icing sugar. Quickly pour onto top of the cake. Allow frosting to set before removing the waxed paper. Stand overnight before cutting into slices.

RICH FRUIT CAKE

5 1/4 lb (2.25 kg) mixed dried fruits
2/3 cup (5 fl oz, 170 ml) port, marsala, or sweet sherry
4 oz (125 g) blanched almonds, chopped
8 oz (300 g) butter, softened
2 2/3 cups (14 1/2 oz, 470 g) brown sugar
2 tablespoons light corn syrup (golden syrup)
2 teaspoons grated lemon rind
8 eggs
5 cups (20 oz, 625 g) all-purpose (plain) flour
1 cup (4 oz, 125 g) self-raising flour
1/2 teaspoon ground dried ginger
1/2 teaspoon ground cinnamon
1/2 teaspoon grated nutmeg
1/2 teaspoon baking soda (bicarbonate of soda)
1/2 teaspoon salt
extra port, marsala, or sweet sherry, as required

Combine fruits in a non-metal bowl, chopping larger pieces into small pieces. Add the alcohol and stir well to mix. Set aside for 10 to 12 hours, stirring from time to time.

Preheat oven to 300°F (150°C, Gas Mark 2). Line a deep-sided 10 to 11 inch (25 to 28 cm) cake pan, and grease it thoroughly.

Add the almonds to the fruit and stir through.

In a large bowl, beat butter and brown sugar until creamy. Add corn syrup and lemon rind, beat thoroughly. Add eggs one at a time, beating well after each addition. At this stage use your hand for further mixing.

In a separate bowl, sift the flours with the spices, baking soda, and salt. Sift half of this into the butter-egg mixture; add half the fruit mixture, and mix. Add the remaining flour and fruit mixtures and fold in, mixing lightly but thoroughly to blend all the ingredients together. Add extra port if required.

Spoon mixture into the cake pan and smooth the surface with a wet hand. Put in the oven and bake for 1 hour. Then reduce the temperature to 250–275°F (120–130°C, Gas Mark 1/2 –1) and continue baking for about 4 more hours, depending on the size and depth of the cake.

Remove from the oven, cover loosely, and let cool slowly in the cake pan. When quite cold, turn out carefully and wrap for storing. It should be stored for 2 to 3 weeks before icing and decorating.

SACHERTORTE

5 oz (150 g) semi-sweet (plain) chocolate
5 oz (150 g) superfine (caster) sugar
4 oz (125 g) butter
4 eggs, separated
few drops vanilla extract (essence)
3 oz (90 g) all-purpose (plain flour)
1/4 level teaspoon double-acting baking powder (1/2 level teaspoon baking powder)
10 oz (300 g) apricot jam or apricot preserve

CHOCOLOLATE ICING:

6 oz (175 g) semi-sweet (plain) chocolate
1 cup (6 fl oz/175 ml) water
1 heaped tablespoon butter
4 oz (125 g) superfine (caster) sugar

Grease and line the base of a 8 1/2 inch (22 cm) spring form cake pan with non stick parchment (baking paper) and lightly dust with flour.

Melt the chocolate in a heatproof bowl over a pan of gently simmering water. Cream the sugar and butter together until very light and fluffy and pale. Beat in the egg yolks one at a time, followed by half the flour, then fold in the remaining egg whites and flour.

Pour into the cake pan, level the top and cook in a very moderate oven (325°F/170°C/Gas Mark 3) for 1–1 1/4 hours until well risen, firm to the touch and skewer inserted in the cake comes out clean. Turn out onto a wire rack.

Melt the chocolate for the icing with 2 tablespoons of water in a heatproof bowl over a pan of gently simmering water. Stir in the butter until melted. Boil the rest of the water with the sugar until at the thread stage (221°F, 104°C) Pour over the chocolate and beat until smooth. Cool, beating from time to time until thick.

When cold, split the cake in half horizontally and fill with half the jam. Reassemble the cake and stand on a serving plate or cake board and spread all over with the remaining jam.

Place 4 tablespoons of icing in a piping bag with a star nozzle. Carefully pour remaining icing over the cake and spread to cover the sides and top evenly. Pipe decorative swirls on top of the cake and decorate with gold cachous. Leave to set before serving.

SHERRIED CHOCOLATE RING

MAKES 1 CAKE

¹/₂ cup (4 fl oz, 125 ml) boiling water
¹/₂ cup (2 oz, 60 g) chopped dried apricots
¹/₂ cup (3 oz, 90 g) chopped seedless raisins
¹/₄ cup (2 fl oz, 60 ml) sweet sherry
4 oz (125 g) butter or margarine, softened
³/₄ cup (6 oz, 185 g) superfine (caster) sugar
2 eggs
3 oz (90 g) unsweetened (cooking) chocolate, melted
2 cups (8 oz, 250 g) self-raising flour
¹/₄ teaspoon salt
¹/₄ teaspoon baking soda (bicarbonate of soda)
¹/₂ cup (4 fl oz, 125 ml) milk

HONEYED CHOCOLATE FROSTING:

1 oz (30 g) butter or margarine
1 tablespoon honey
3 oz (90 g) unsweetened (cooking) chocolate, grated
1 ¹/₂ cups (8 oz, 250 g) confectioners' (icing) sugar, sifted
2–3 teaspoons lemon juice

In a bowl pour boiling water over the apricots; let stand a few minutes, then pour off the liquid. Add raisins and sweet sherry to the apricots, and set aside for 1 hour.

Preheat oven to 325°F (160°C, Gas Mark 3). Thoroughly grease and flour an 8 inch (20 cm) fluted ring tin.

Beat butter and sugar until creamy. Add eggs one at a time, beating well after each addition, then beat the cooled chocolate through. Sift dry ingredients over butter-chocolate mixture; fold through lightly. Then add apricot-raisin mixture and milk; fold in lightly but thoroughly to combine. Spoon into the fluted ring tin.

Bake for 55 to 60 minutes. Remove from oven and stand for 5 to 6 minutes before turning out onto a cake rack to cool.

When cold, drizzle honeyed chocolate frosting over the top and allow it to run unevenly down the flutes or grooves in the cake.

Honeyed chocolate frosting: Combine butter, honey, and chocolate in a heatproof basin and heat over hot, not boiling, water until well blended. Remove from the heat and allow to cool slightly.

Gradually add confectioners' sugar, beating well; then add lemon juice. Spoon mixture over the cake and swirl or mark into an attractive design. Allow to set before cutting.

SUGAR PLUM CAKE

SERVES 12

1 cup (7 oz, 220 g) pitted (stoned) dessert prunes
1/2 cup (4 oz, 125 g) unsalted butter or margarine
1/2 cup (4 oz, 125 g) superfine (caster) sugar
2 x 2 oz (60 g) eggs
1 1/4 cups (5 oz, 155 g) self-raising flour
2/3 cup (4 oz, 125 g) semolina
1/2 cup (2 1/2 fl oz, 75 ml) orange juice

SYRUP:

1/2 cup (4 fl oz, 125 ml) water
3 tablespoons superfine (caster) sugar
1 teaspoon orange flower water

Cover prunes with boiling water, leave for 10 minutes to plump up then drain well. Cream butter with sugar until light and fluffy. Add eggs, one at a time, beating well after each addition. Sift in flour, add semolina and orange juice and stir gently until combined.

Put two-thirds of mixture in a lined and greased 8 inch (20 cm) cake tin, spread smooth. Arrange prunes in a circle on top, then spread remaining mixture over smoothly.

Bake at 350°F (180°C, Gas Mark 4) for 50 minutes or until cooked. Cool on a wire cooling tray.

Syrup: Put water and sugar in a saucepan and stir over heat until dissolved. Alternatively dissolve in a microwave oven on HIGH for 1 minute. Stir in orange flower water. Stand cake on cooling tray over a large plate and pour hot syrup over warm cake. Carefully transfer moist cake to a serving plate before serving.

WHOLEWHEAT (WHOLEMEAL) CARROT CAKE

1 cup (8 oz, 250 g) sugar, very slightly warmed
³/4 cup (6 fl oz, 180 ml) maize oil
2 eggs
1 1/2 cups (12 oz, 375 g) grated carrot
1 cup (4 oz, 125 g) wholewheat (wholemeal) flour
1/2 teaspoon double-acting baking powder (1 teaspoon baking powder)
1/2 teaspoon ground ginger
1 1/2 teaspoon grated nutmeg
1/4 teaspoon salt
³/4 cup (4 oz, 125 g) chopped seedless raisins
1/2 cup (2 oz, 60 g) chopped walnuts
1 teaspoon grated orange rind

CREAM CHEESE FROSTING:

4 oz (125 g) packet cream cheese
2 oz (60 g) butter or margarine
1 teaspoon grated orange rind
1 1/2 cups (8 oz, 250 g) confectioners' (icing) sugar, sifted

Preheat oven to 350°F (180°C, Gas Mark 4). Line and grease an 8 x 4 1/2 inch (20 x 12 cm) loaf tin.

Beat sugar and oil together until well mixed. Add eggs one at a time, beating well after each addition; then add grated carrot and mix well.

Sift dry ingredients together. Put raisins, walnuts, and orange rind in another bowl, and sift the flour mixture over them; toss well to mix. Fold this into the sugar-carrot mixture, mixing lightly but thoroughly. Spoon into the loaf tin.

Bake for 35 to 40 minutes. Remove from oven and stand for 3 to 4 minutes before turning out onto a cake rack to cool.

Cream cheese frosting: Stand the cream cheese and butter at room temperature until softened. Put in a bowl with the orange rind and beat until creamy. Gradually add the sugar, beating well between each addition.

Spread onto the cake, using a knife to swirl into an attractive design. Let it firm before cutting.

ZUCCHINI (COURGETTE) & ORANGE CAKE

SERVES 12

¹/₂ cup (4 oz, 125 g) unsalted butter or margarine
¹/₂ cup (4 oz, 125 g) raw sugar
3 x 2 oz (60 g) eggs, separated
1 teaspoon vanilla extract (essence)
1 cup grated zucchini (courgette), firmly packed
finely grated rind of 1 orange
1 cup (4 oz, 125 g) self-raising wholewheat (wholemeal) flour, sifted
1–2 tablespoons sunflower kernels

SYRUP:

¹/₂ cup (4 oz, 125 g) vanilla or superfine (caster) sugar
¹/₂ cup (4 fl oz, 125 ml) orange juice

Beat butter and sugar together until light and fluffy. Add egg yolks, one at a time, and beat well after each addition. Stir in vanilla, zucchini, and orange rind. Whisk egg whites until stiff. Gently fold flour into mixture in three batches, alternating with stiff egg white.

Spoon mixture in a base-lined and greased 8 inch (20 cm) round cake tin. Sprinkle with sunflower kernels. Bake at 350°F (180°C, Gas Mark 4) for 40 minutes or until cooked. Test with a warm skewer.

Syrup: Dissolve sugar in orange juice. Pour over cake when it comes out of oven. Leave to cool in tin before removing.

Serve with orange segments and natural yogurt or cream cheese.

BLUE RIBBON SPONGE SANDWICH

3 eggs
¹/₂ cups (4 oz, 125 g) superfine (caster) sugar
1 cup (4 oz, 125 g) all-purpose (plain) flour
1 tablespoon cornstarch (cornflour)
1 teaspoon double-acting baking powder (2 teaspoons baking powder)
¹/₄ teaspoon salt
2 teaspoons butter or margarine
¹/₄ cup (2 fl oz, 60 ml) very hot water
¹/₂ teaspoon vanilla extract (essence)
raspberry jelly (jam)

Preheat oven to 350°F (180°C, Gas Mark 4). Grease two deep 7 inch (18 cm) sandwich tins and dust lightly with flour.

Separate the eggs and put the whites in a clean, dry, preferably glass bowl; beat with an electric beater, hand-beater or egg whisk to stiff white foam. Add the sugar, 1 tablespoon at a time and beat well after each addition — the sugar must be completely dissolved. Fold in the egg yolks lightly and gently.

Sift flour with cornstarch, baking powder, and salt twice. Then sift again over the egg mixture (don't mix it in yet).

Melt butter in hot water, add the vanilla extract, and carefully pour down the side of the bowl into the egg mixture. Using a metal spoon and with a gentle folding motion, mix dry ingredients and liquid through the eggs and sugar. Pour mixture gently into the two sandwich tins, being careful to avoid harshly knocking or banging either the bowl or the tins. Spread lightly to even the surface.

Bake for 22 to 25 minutes, preferably both tins on the same oven shelf so that both sponges will be evenly cooked and browned. Remove from oven and stand for 1 minute, out of a draught, then turn carefully onto a fine mesh cake rack or a kitchen towel over a cake rack to cool.

Fill with raspberry jelly and dust the top with sifted icing confectioners' sugar.

Strawberry Sponge: Fill and top with fresh whipped cream and decorate the top with whole or sliced strawberries.

COFFEE GÂTEAU

18 sponge fingers
sherry or brandy
4 oz (125 g) butter
$^2/_3$ cup (4 oz, 125 g) superfine (caster) sugar
2 eggs
2 tablespoons very strong black coffee
10 fl oz (300 ml) cream
grated chocolate and walnuts for decoration

Line a pudding basin with sponge fingers and sprinkle well with sherry or brandy.

Cream butter and sugar until light and fluffy. Add lightly beaten eggs very slowly, beating continuously. Then add the black coffee very slowly while beating continuously (if coffee is added too quickly the mixture will curdle). Pour into sponge-lined basin and cover with more sponge fingers. Cover with greased aluminum foil. Place a plate with a weight on top. Chill for several hours before serving.

To serve, turn coffee gâteau out onto a serving plate, cover with whipped cream and decorate with grated chocolate and walnuts.

CONTINENTAL CREAM SPONGE

MAKES 1 CAKE

2 eggs
1 cup (8 oz, 250 g) superfine (caster) sugar, slightly warmed
1 teaspoon vanilla essence
2 cups (8 oz, 250 g) all-purpose (plain) flour
2 teaspoons baking powder
¹/₄ teaspoon salt
10 fl oz (300 ml) thick cream, lightly whipped
confectioner's (icing) sugar, for topping

HAZELNUT FILLING:

1¹/₄ cups (10 fl oz, 300 ml) cream
¹/₂ cup (4 oz, 125 g) superfine (caster) sugar
³/₄ cup (3 oz, 90 g) finely chopped filberts (hazelnuts)
6 egg yolks
2–3 teaspoons brandy or rum

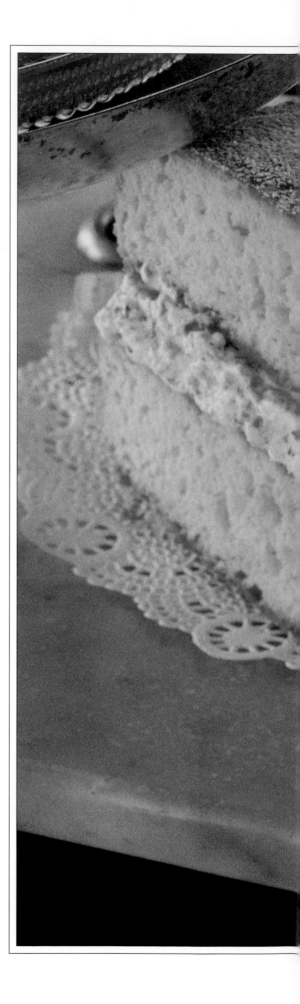

Preheat oven to 325°F (160°C, Gas Mark 3). Grease and flour a 9 inch (23 cm) square slab tin.

Beat the eggs until very frothy. Gradually add the warmed superfine sugar, beating each addition until well dissolved and then add the vanilla essence with the last addition of sugar.

Sift the flour, baking powder, and salt together. Sift about half of this over the egg-sugar mixture and fold through gently. Add about half of the lightly whipped cream and fold through gently. Repeat the flour and cream addition with the remaining mixtures — do not overmix. Spoon into the slab tin. Bake for 55 to 60 minutes. Turn out carefully onto a cake rack to cool.

Hazelnut filling: Place the cream, sugar and filberts (hazelnuts) in a small nonstick saucepan; bring slowly to a boil, then simmer over low heat until the mixture is thick — approximately 10 minutes.

Remove from the heat, pour the mixture into a heatproof bowl (warmed slightly), and stir until cold.

Add the egg yolks one at a time and beat in thoroughly; add brandy or rum. Spread onto the layers of cake, rejoin the layers and cover the outside of the cake as desired.

Cut the cake in half and sandwich together with the filling; dust sifted confectioner's sugar over the top. Chill slightly, before serving in slices.

RICH MOCHA CREAM GÂTEAU

12 oz (375 g) unsweetened (cooking) chocolate, chopped
1 cup (8 fl oz, 250 ml) milk
2 oz (60 g) butter or margarine, softened well
1 3/4 cups (7 oz, 220 g) all-purpose (plain) flour
1/2 teaspoon double-acting baking powder (1 teaspoon baking powder)
2 teaspoons instant coffee powder
1/2 teaspoon baking soda (bicarbonate of soda)
1/4 teaspoon salt
1 cup (7 oz, 220 g) superfine (caster) sugar
3 eggs, beaten
2 teaspoons rum extract (essence) or brandy extract (essence)

FILLING:

10 oz (315 g) heavy (double) cream, chilled
1 tablespoon confectioners' (icing) sugar

FROSTING:

6 oz (185 g) unsweetened (cooking) chocolate, chopped
4 oz (150 g) unsalted butter, softened
2 egg yolks
1 teaspoon instant coffee powder
1 teaspoon rum extract (essence) or brandy extract (essence)
1 1/4 – 1 1/2 cups (6 1/2 – 7 1/2 oz, 200–230 g) confectioners' (icing) sugar, sifted

Preheat oven to 350°F (180°C, Gas Mark 4). Line the bottoms of two 9 inch (23 cm) layer pans, and grease well.

Melt chocolate in a heatproof bowl over hot water; set aside to cool slightly. When cool, combine with milk and softened butter. Sift dry ingredients into a large bowl and make a well in the middle; add the combined chocolate, milk, and butter and beat for 1 to 2 minutes. Add beaten eggs and extract, and beat for 2 minutes. Spoon into the pans.

Bake for 25 to 30 minutes. Remove from oven and stand for 2 to 3 minutes, then carefully turn out onto cake racks to cool. When cold, slice each cake in half horizontally — making four layers.

Filling: Whip the cream and sugar until thickened. Chill well.

Frosting: Melt chocolate in heatproof bowl over hot water. Cool to room temperature. Blend the chocolate into the creamed butter, add egg yolks and coffee powder and beat well. Add the extract and sugar to make a smooth consistency.

To assemble: Spread whipped cream between the four cake layers and re-form into a gâteau, pressing gently to adhere. Spoon half the frosting on top of the gâteau and use remainder for decoration in swirls or rosettes, as desired. Chill before serving.

SWISS (JELLY) ROLL

³/4 cup (3 oz, 90 g) self-raising flour
pinch salt
3 eggs
³/4 cup (4¹/2 oz, 140 g) superfine (caster) sugar
1 tablespoon hot water
3–4 tablespoons warm jam
superfine (caster) sugar for dredging
whipped cream

Grease a 15 x 11 x 1 inch (38 x 28 x 2.5 cm) Swiss (jelly) roll tin and line with waxed (greaseproof) greased paper. Set oven temperature at 400°F (200°C, Gas Mark 6). Sift the flour with the salt. Place the eggs and sugar in a bowl and stand over a pan of gently simmering, not boiling, water. Whisk well until the mixture is very thick and creamy.

Remove the bowl from the heat and continue whisking until the mixture is cool. Fold in the flour as lightly as possible then the hot water. Pour the mixture into the prepared tin. Bake for 7 to 10 minutes until pale golden. Do not overcook as it makes rolling up difficult.

Quickly turn the sponge out onto a kitchen (tea) towel, well sprinkled with superfine sugar. Trim off the crisp edges, roll in the towel, cool then unroll.

Spread with jam and whipped cream. Roll up. Sprinkle with a little more superfine sugar before serving.

Published by Harbour Books
PO Box 48, Millers Point NSW 2000, Australia

First published in 1996
Reprinted 1997

ISBN 1 86302 507 3